No Plays Exchanged. *Price, 15 Cents.*

SPENCER'S UNIVERSAL STAGE. No. 54.

BOUQUET.

A Comedietta, in One Act.

ADAPTED FROM THE FRENCH

BY J. A. WOODWARD.

BOSTON:
CHARLES H. SPENCER,
149 WASHINGTON STREET.

BOUQUET.

A Commedietta,

IN ONE ACT.

ADAPTED FROM THE FRENCH,

BY

J. A. WOODWARD.

BOSTON:
CHARLES H. SPENCER, Agent,
149 Washington Street.

BOUQUET.

CHARACTERS.

PAUL GAILLARD.

BICOQUET.

JENNIE GAILLARD.

PAULINE.

SCENE LAID IN PARIS.

TIME. — The present.

BOUQUET.

SCENE. *Elegant Salon in* GAILLARD'S *house.* — *Doors* C. *and at* R. 1 E. — *Door at* L. 3 E. — *Window* R. — *Fireplace and mantel* L. *at back.* — *Piano* L. 1 E. — *Oval centre-table centre of stage.* — *Two chairs.* — *Work-table* R., *and sofa near.* — *Bookcase* L. 2 E.

JENNIE *discovered seated at piano.* — GAILLARD *preparing to go out.*

Gaillard (*to himself, seeking what he needs*). My coat, my hat, my umbrella — my handkerchief.

Jennie (*sighing*). Go, then, if you must.

Gail. Now you must know that if it were not absolutely necessary ——

Jennie. *I'm* not sure of it at all — but that makes no difference. I *am* sure that you've not passed a single evening at home for a week.

Gail. Not one?

Jennie. Not one! And you never take me anywhere; and I'm dying to see the new play at the theatre.

Gail. We'll go next week.

Jennie (*wearily*). Ah!

Gail. Now do be sensible, and try to understand me. The money market — the financial situation — I am obliged to be continually on the alert, or else ——

Jennie. I can't see why the money market should take you to the opera every evening.

Gail. Yes! I go to hear the rumors and news, in order to profit by it to gain money enough to lavish on my little wife.

Jennie. What I'm going to ask you for won't require much money. On your way down town please buy me a bouquet — a pretty bouquet. Will you remember it?

Gail. Indeed I will. Bye, bye, Jennie dear.

Jennie. Shall you return late?

Gail. No; about half past ten or eleven — as usual. Bye, bye, dear! (*Crosses towards door,* C.)

Jennie. Bye, bye. Don't forget my bouquet.

Gail. (*exit door,* C.). Yes — a bouquet! a pretty, large bouquet.

Jennie (*rising and crossing* R.). What a trouble it must be for him to have a little wife — like myself — and to leave her here for a week — all alone. I know that it's to earn money, so that I can have all I wish, as he says — and really I have a great deal — but I should like more. (*Sits near table and takes needle-work.*) I must think of some way to pass the evening. It's a long time till eleven o'clock. O, Penelope! Penelope! (*Leaves her work and takes newspaper.*) What could Penelope have read when she was tired of work. (*Glances at paper.*) Where was I? (*Reading.*) "Mons. Legrand was desperate! The policeman tore his hair." (*Violent ringing.*) Who's that? I don't expect any one. It's Paul! doubtless he has forgotten something.

Enter PAULINE, C.

Pauline. Madame!

Jennie. Well?

Pauline. It's a young man, madame.

Jennie. A young man?

Bicoquet (*passes his head into door,* C., *and trying to attract* PAULINE'S *attention*). Here! I say! young woman! here!

Pauline. Sir?

Bic. (*stage whisper*). Don't say a young man — say a man still young — that is more exact.

Jennie. But, sir ——

Bic. A thousand pardons, madame. I only showed myself to correct a mistake. I know very well that until madame has said "Admit the gentleman," I ought to remain here in the passage. I return, madame — I return. (*Disappears.*)

Jennie (*rising*). What is the gentleman's name? Did he give his name?

Pauline. His name?

Bic. (*reappearing — to* PAULINE, *as before*). Here, you, the card.

Jennie. Again?

Bic. A thousand pardons, madame! She forgets that I have given her my card. I have shown myself to recall it to her. I return, madame — I return. (*Disappears.*)

Pauline. Yes, madame, here is his card. (*Gives card.*)

Jennie (*reading card*). "Jules Bicoquet." I don't know him at all.

Bic. (*reappearing, impatiently*). Tell her what I told you. (*Disappears.*)

Pauline (*to* B.). I was going to tell her in a moment. (*To* JENNIE.) This gentleman said that he called about a very urgent matter which particularly interested madame.

Bic. (*opening door, without showing himself*). And which will not admit of a moment's delay. (*Shuts door.*)

Jennie. What can this mean? I must attend to it. Show the gentleman in.

PAULINE *opens door, and signals to* B. *to enter.*

Bic. (*majestic entrance*). At last! (*Advancing and bowing.*) Madame!

Jennie. Sir! (*To* PAULINE, *who crosses towards door,* R.) Remain, Pauline.

Bic. Ah, madame, five minutes only — I beg of you — just five minutes.

Jennie. But, sir ——

Bic. You will not repent it.

Jennie (*aside*). What should I fear, after all? He appears strange, but not dangerous. (*To* PAULINE.) You may go, Pauline.

[*Exit* PAULINE, C.

Bic. Whatever I may appear, madame, I have at least one of the qualities which distinguish superior men — I have only one, perhaps ——

Jennie. And that is ——

Bic. I am stupid with the ladies.

Jennie. Sir!

Bic. Ah! you will not believe me: *thanks* — but I will soon convince you of it. My name is easy to pronounce — James Bicoquet. My age — thirty-four years. As to my fortune — it is sufficient. Fifteen years ago, it would have passed as quite handsome, but to-day — in modern Paris ——

Jennie. I beg your pardon, sir, but ——

Bic. Madame!

Jennie. You said this interview concerned a matter which interested me particularly.

Bic. Yes, madame!

Jennie. And I would like to know.

Bic. What! Immediately?

Jennie. Yes! Immediately!

Bic. I will not conceal that I intended to keep it until the last — but since you seem to desire it — your husband deceives you, madame!

Jennie. Sir!

Bic. You are the most interesting and most unhappy of lovely wives — your husband deceives you!

Jennie. Sir! Sir!

Bic. At this moment, even, he is above. (*Points to ceiling.*)

Jennie (*looking at ceiling*). Above?

Bic. Yes, above, with the little actress on the second flight. He is just sitting down to a game of Bezique — and he is losing. I can't see the cards — but for all that, I'll wager that he loses.

Jennie (*fiercely*). Proofs, sir — proofs!

Bic. Do you ask for proofs?

Jennie. Yes!

Bic. Very well. (*Shows the hat which he holds in his hands.*) Look at this, madame! Have the kindness to look. (*Puts hat on his head, which disappears completely.*)

Jennie. Well?

Bic. Well — don't you see? (*Takes off hat and holds it in his hand.*)

Jennie. What does that prove?

Bic. That — that proves it is not my hat. It proves it belongs to Mons. Paul Gaillard. (*Shows inside of hat.*) P. G., madame — P. G.!

Jennie. Too true!

Bic. Ten minutes ago, madame, *I* was above there. What a recollection — and I was forced to leave to make room for your husband. Instead of taking my own hat, I took his, and I have brought it to you. Are you convinced now? Is the proof sufficient? (*Puts hat on table.*)

Jennie (*falls, overwhelmed, on sofa near work-table*). O heavens! can this be true?

Bic. (*melancholy, and taking chair* R. *of table*). Every evening, at nine o'clock, I come and sit near her. (*Sits.*)

Jennie. But, sir!

Bic. (*firmly, and rising*). Ah! Now that I have proved that I really have something interesting to say to you, I hope that you will have the goodness not to interrupt me, and that you will allow me to relate my little story. (*Reseating himself, sadly.*) Every evening, at nine o'clock, I come and sit near her. "Good evening, To-to," I say to her. "Toto" diminutive for Antonia. "Good evening, Co-co," she replies. "Coco" diminutive for Bicoquet. "How de do, Toto." "O, not badly, Coco; bring out the cards." And then I bring out the cards, and the play commences. Forty for the trump — one hundred for the ace — two hundred and fifty — five hundred. O! so complete, so intense a happiness, could not last. A week ago I came — I rang — and the servant stopped me, and said: "You must not enter, sir — madame is with her godmother from Normandy." I went away without a word. The next day I returned. The godmother was again there. The next day the godmother was there still, and I became suspicious. I played the spy, and I discovered that this godmother, who had taken my place, and interrupted my happiness, was ——

Jennie (*angrily*). My husband! My husband with that woman?

Bic. (*approaching his chair*). If we leave him there ——

Jennie (*rising, and crosses quickly*). What did you say?

Bic. (*rising*). I can see but two solutions to the matter. If your husband keeps my place, that he has taken — why, then, I must take his. (*Sadly.*) Every evening, at nine o'clock, I will come.

Jennie (*indignantly*). Sir! what do you mean?

Bic. I know it's rather strange; but if you were a true Parisian, say of 1852 — you see — I do not complain. In the first place, I have one flight up stairs less to climb, and also you are far more pretty than — (*suddenly*) have you, any cards?

Jennie (*very indignant*). Sir, leave the room instantly!

Bic. No? that does not suit you. Well, then, the second solution is — we must call your husband down.

Jennie. Ah! I much prefer that.

Bic. When he comes down, I will go up. It's very simple, and everything will be proper. Gaillard here — Bicoquet there. (*Points above.*) Yes, we must call your husband down.

Jennie. I ask nothing more — but how?

Bic. As you wish.

Jennie. Give me an idea.

Bic. (*violently*). And why should I furnish you with ideas. It seems to me that you are interested as much as I.

Jennie (*equally violent*). And how can I, in the state of excitement in which I am?

Bic. (*still more violent*). Well, madame, and I. Do you suppose that I am not excited myself? So much so that I could scream — if I did not think it too familiar for a first visit. (*Sound of piano and singing heard overhead.*) There! hear that? (*The voice stops and air continues* — Bic. *sings.*) La — la — la!

Jennie. What has happened to you?

Bic. That air — I remember it. She always sings so when she wins. Ah! (*Sings.*) La — la — la! I assure you, madame, that if that air continues, I shall certainly scream. (*Goes behind table and screams.*)

Jennie (*crosses quickly to fireplace*). I beg of you to remain quiet, sir. (*Rings.*)

Bic. Do you turn me away, madame?

Jennie. No; an idea has just struck me.

Bic. To call him down?

Jennie. Yes.

Enter Pauline, c.

Pauline (*at door*, c.). Madame?

Jennie. Go up stairs, one flight, to Mademoiselle — (*to* Bic.) What name did you say, sir?

Bic. (*with an effort*). Antonia Brunet.

Jennie. To Mademoiselle Antonia Brunet. You must say that I am suffering — that Madame Gaillard is suffering. Be sure and pronounce the *name distinctly* — and that the music makes me worse.

Pauline. Is madame ill?

Jennie. Yes — no — what matters it to you? Go — the name — don't forget — Madame Gaillard — say the name loud and distinctly — scream so that all can hear you. [*Exit* Pauline, c.

Bic. I understand you. You count upon his heart.

Jennie. And I am not wrong, for he *is* good; and when he knows — when he believes that I am ill ——

Bic. He will come down. It's possible, after all. (*Music stops.*) There, the music stops. The errand is done.

Jennie. Quick, then! Go, sir — go!

Bic. O! we have five minutes still.

Jennie. He has only one flight to descend.

Bic. Ah, you don't understand your husband, madame — you don't know him. He is an adept at deception.

Jennie. How?

Bic. Do you imagine that he will come directly here, at the risk of being caught? No, indeed! This house has two doors — one to the Rue de la Porte, and the other to the Rue Lafayette. Don't you see? Mons. Gaillard will descend the back stairs, pass around the house — enter the front door — leisurely ascend the front stairs. It will take at least five minutes. Allowing that his anxiety for your health should quicken his steps to-day, he ought to be now — (*looks out of window.*) What did I tell you, madame? Here he is!

Jennie. Take care, he may see you!

Bic. No fear, madame! (*Draws back from window, still looking.*) He has my hat in one hand, and a bouquet in the other.

Jennie. A large bouquet of roses?

Bic. Yes.

Jennie. I asked him to buy me one.

Bic. (*laughing and coming down front*). You asked him to — ha! ha! He is an adept. Why, I recognized that bouquet.

Jennie. You recognized it?

Bic. Perfectly. The very moment that I came out from above, there, a great brute of a servant brought it in the name of young — what d'ye call him — no matter who. Your husband bought it of mademoiselle's maid, who appropriates all the bouquets.

Jennie (*indignantly*). O!

Bic. But here he comes, madame — I must go. Adieu, madame. (*Crosses to table.*)

Jennie. Adieu, sir. Do be quick.

Bic. I leave you your husband's hat, madame. He will bring you mine, which you will have the kindness to send to me — will you not?

Jennie. But where, sir?

Bic. Where? Why, above, certainly. Where do you think I am going?

Jennie. Very well, sir. It shall be sent to you.

Bic. And, I beg of you, give orders that it shall be delivered to the servant who opens the door. It will not be necessary to call me personally. (*False exit*, C.)

Jennie (*stopping him*). This way, sir. Pauline will show you out.

Bic. Adieu, madame — perhaps we may never meet again.

Jennie (*aside*). I certainly hope not.

Bic. Adieu — be happy — as for me — I will try — adieu, madame. [*Exit door*, R.

Jennie. First, I must conceal the hat. (*Opens door*, R., *and puts hat in her room.*) And now for my revenge. At first I must be sweet, and patient, and hypocritical. That will throw him off guard, and then —— (*while speaking, she has seated herself as before the entrance of* BIC.)

Enter GAILLARD, C., *with bouquet and hat in hand.*

Gail. Suffering? What can be the matter? (*Puts hat on table, and also bouquet.*)

Jennie (*sighs*). Ah!

Gail. Jennie, dear Jennie!

Jennie (*sweetly*). Is it you, my dear? I thought that you would not return till half past ten or eleven, as usual.

Gail. Yes; but when I am away from you, you know ——

Jennie. You are always kind. But the stocks, and the money market — you must not neglect them.

Gail. O! I was going to tell you — I have been in luck — I had the good fortune to meet Mons. Magimel.

Jennie (*sadly*). Is he well?

Gail. Quite well; and he gave me all the information that I desired. So I had an opportunity to return quickly.

Jennie (*sarcastically*). Quickly!

Gail. Yes, as quickly as I could; and that is why ——

Jennie. You took time to purchase a bouquet, however.

Gail. You knew I would, since you requested it.

Jennie. Give it to me.

Gail. (*presenting bouquet*). Isn't it pretty?

Jennie (*takes bouquet and crosses*). It's superb — it must have cost you dear.

Gail. (*thoughtlessly*). Yes, it cost me two hundred francs.

Jennie. Two hundred francs?

Gail. (*recovering himself*). Twenty francs — I meant twenty francs.

Jennie (*examining bouquet, and putting it on piano*). Did you buy it at the opera?

Gail. (*embarrassed*). No, I bought it in the Rue Lafitte. Magimel and I, while chatting, strolled to the Rue Lafitte, so while I was there —— (*Aside.*) It's lucky I noticed the florist's address.

Jennie (*aside*). "Coco" was right. He *is* an adept.

Gail. And now that I've returned so soon, I must tell you frankly ——

Jennie. Frankly?

Gail. Why, yes. I had a presentiment — just now — that is, when I left you this evening — it seemed to me — I thought I saw — that you did not look as well as usual.

Jennie. What, am I ugly?

Gail. How can you say such a thing — you were very handsome — you always are — but you seemed a little — you are not ill, are you? Have you been ill since I went away?

Jennie. Yes.

Gail. Ah! my heart told me so. What is the matter, Jennie?

Jennie. I cannot tell you — a little nervous.

Gail. Yes — I'm so sorry.

Jennie. I was nervous a quarter of an hour ago, and I did something that I am afraid you will scold me for, if I tell you.

Gail. No, no! I will not scold.

Jennie (*cutting her words*). The person who lives overhead — do you know who that person is?

Gail. (*slyly*). Who lives overhead?

Jennie. Yes.

Gail. (*same*). A marine insurance agent, I believe.

Jennie (*observing him*). No, I mean a lady.

Gail. (*same*). An old lady?

Jennie. No, a young lady — she sat down to the piano just now and began to sing — I don't know what she was singing — but I was so nervous, so excited, that I could not contain myself. I sent Pauline to request this lady to discontinue her song. Was I wrong?

Gail. No, you were perfectly right.

Jennie. Thanks, you are very good. (*Takes bouquet, and crosses to table.*)

Gail. Where are you going?

Jennie. To carry this bouquet into my room. (*Stops at table, and takes up* B.'s *hat.*) Why, what kind of a hat have you got? (*Examining it.*) That isn't yours.

Gail. What — isn't it? (*Tries on hat, which is too small.*) No, it is not mine.

Jennie. Let me see it. (*Takes it.*) No, nor it isn't Magimel's.

Gail. Indeed.

Jennie (*shows him inside of hat*). J. B., my dear — J. B. That doesn't stand for Magimel.

Gail. (*after having looked into hat — confused*). No, it's not Magimel's. I didn't say that it was, did I.

Jennie. No, you did not *say* so; but if it does not belong to him, whose is it?

Gail. (*thinking a moment — both come forward same order*). Ah! I know. The explanation is very simple. It could not be simpler, and at the same time it is quite comical. (*Forced laugh.*)

Jennie. But tell me, and let me enjoy it.

Gail. Yes, but it's so comical. You see, I was in a hurry to return here — anxious on your account, my dear — and I ran. Well, as I was running, I encountered a gentleman who was also running in an opposite direction. You are listening to me?

Jennie. Yes.

Gail. Now just let me show you — to make it more clear. (*Bus. of running against man — crosses,* R.) You see the two hats were thrown upon the ground — one here, the other there. I picked one up, without looking, apologized to the gentleman, and as I was in a hurry, I came away with a hat which did not belong to me. (*Forced laugh.*) You see it's very simple.

Jennie. Yes, yes — I see. (*Aside.*) He is *decidedly* an adept; but I will force him to acknowledge yet.

Gail. (*examining hat*). But I've made a good exchange. This is newer than mine.

Jennie (*takes bouquet which she has left on table*). I will be back in a moment, my dear. I am going to carry my bouquet into my room. Now don't run away while I'm gone — will you?

Gail. Could you believe such a thing?

Jennie. I will return immediately. [*Exit door* R., *with bouquet.*

Gail. Stay here! I think I will. She nearly caught me that time — and all on account of that miserable hat. Yes, my wife is pretty, sweet, and agreeable, and the best thing I can do is to stay at home and take care of her.

Enter PAULINE, C.

Pauline. A letter, sir!

Gail. A letter?

Pauline. From the lady above, sir.

Gail. (*dissimulating*). The lady above — I don't know her!

Pauline. Possibly, sir; but she sent you this letter.

Gail. (*taking letter*). She does wrong to write to me — very wrong.

Pauline. But she said that it must be delivered to you, even if madame were present.

Gail Did she say that?

Pauline. That's what she said, sir.

Gail. (*flattered*). Jealousy! But still she is wrong, and I am astonished at such conduct on the part of so distinguished a person. (*Opens letter and reads.*) "You old thief." What? (*Reads again.*) "Old thief, I know that my servants read all my letters, so I will put nothing in this which will compromise you." (*Spoken.*) Thief, indeed! (*Reads.*) "I suppose that you understand me. If you are not in my room in five minutes, I shall know what action to take. Yours — or rather wanting my own — Antonia." (*Repeats.*) "I suppose that you understand me. If you are not in my room in five minutes, I shall know what action to take." (*Spoken.*) This is some joke, but I really don't understand it.

Pauline. Well, sir.

Gail. What?

Pauline. Why, the reply — she is waiting.

Gail. There is no reply.

Pauline. Very well, sir. [*Exit,* C.

Gail. (*to* PAULINE *during exit*). Say it very politely — add that I laughed very much. (*Returns down,* C.) That will please her, and I do not wish to offend her — but it is a strange joke. I cannot understand it. There ought to be some point to a jest. For instance, if you were to approach a gentleman whom you don't know, and ask him to hold one end of a long string, and then ask another gentleman, whom you know just as little, to hold the other end — and then walk quietly away. Now that is a good joke, but simply because there is some sense to it. (*Looks at letter.*) But *that!* (*Finishes his monologue at* R.)

Enter PAULINE, C.

Pauline. Sir! Sir!

Gail. Well, what is the matter?

Pauline. That lady ——

Gail. Another letter?

Pauline. She says that you have only three minutes, and that if you don't come up, she'll come down.

Gail. Well, tell her that I cannot come — that I am seriously engaged. Yes — very seriously — in trying to keep quiet. She takes me for a fool, but she is mistaken.

Pauline. Well, sir! [*Exit,* C.

Gail. (*same business for exit*). Tell her so very politely. Now what kind of a scrape am I getting into? Is she really capable of — What in the world are we coming to, if a man cannot make a mistake in a flight of stairs without ——

Pauline (*enters hurriedly,* C.). Sir! Sir!

Gail. Well?

Pauline. She says you have only two minutes, sir, and she is putting on her gloves.

Gail. Well, what of it?

Pauline. I don't know what has happened, sir, or what she accuses you of — but she spoke to me about sending for the police.

Gail. The police?

Pauline. Yes, sir.

Gail. (*furious*). What the devil can be the matter with the woman? What can she mean?

Pauline. I'm only a poor girl, but if I were to advise you, sir, you ought to speak to that lady. There is but little time, sir.

Gail. Yes, yes — I'll go. But tell her so politely.

Pauline. Well, sir. [*Exit.*

Gail. (*puts* BIC.'s *hat on head — seeing that it does not fit, he throws it down savagely on table*). What's that now? Must I be bothered all my life with that hat?

Enter JENNIE, R., *with* GAIL.'s *hat, which she holds behind her.*

Jennie (*extremely dignified*). And now, my dear, I hope you will explain to me how *your* hat —— (*Presents his hat.*)

Gail. (*taking his hat and putting* B.'s *on table*). Ah! thank you. (*Puts it on.*) Just in time. (*Opens door,* C.)

Jennie. What, are you going out?

Gail. Yes ——

Jennie. Why?

Gail. I will explain by and by. [*Exit.*

Jennie (*down* C.). And just as I came in with his hat to confound

— to overwhelm him. And I had prepared such a pretty lecture, and at the end of the lecture a pardon prettier still. (*Furiously.*) But now ——

Enter BICOQUET *desperate.*

Bic. They've turned me out, madame.

Jennie. You?

Bic. Yes! This time they turned me out!

Jennie. You here again, sir?

Bic. Ought you not to expect it, since you have let him go up there again? It's your fault. Why didn't you keep him?

Jennie. Is my husband up there?

Bic. He is madame! So naturally — I ——

Jennie. Proofs, sir, proofs!

Bic. I anticipate them. (*Showing* GAIL.'s *hat.*) Look at that hat.

Jennie. His hat again?

Bic. Precisely.

Jennie. This is too much!

Bic. (*putting hat on table*). And as mine is no longer above, your husband will have to come down bareheaded — when he comes.

Jennie (*exasperated*). And he hadn't been back five minutes — only five minutes.

Bic. How can you help it, madame? Your husband is infatuated.

Jennie (*falls into chair* L. *of table. — Angrily, to herself*). And he is there again. (*Points above — rises.*)

Bic. Yes, madame, he is there, over our heads. (*Indignantly.*) And the floor doesn't open to swallow them. (*Listening.*) We can hear footsteps.

Jennie (*preoccupied*). We must call him down again, sir.

Bic. That's been my sole object since the commencement of our acquaintance; but how?

Jennie. When she sang just now, we heard her. So if we sing here, they must hear us above.

Bic. Very probably, madame, sound having one quality in common with your husband — it ascends.

Jennie. Then sing, sir.

Bic. I?

Jennie. Certainly! It must be a man's voice. Don't you understand? Jealousy.

Bic. But you see I am always enveloped in a blanket for twelve hours before I attempt to sing; and this evening I did not expect ——

Jennie. What difference does it make, provided you sing loud, and that you make noise enough?

Bic. If madame will have the goodness to get me some blankets, I will wrap myself up, and perhaps in twelve hours ——

Jennie. No, no! Now — immediately! Come, come! (*Sits at piano.*)

Bic. You see, madame, that my style of music ——

Jennie (strikes chord). You are losing time. Quick, quick! (BIC. *sings.* — *Enter* GAIL. *frightened, with gray hat on his head. On his entrance,* JENNIE *rises with dignity.* BIC. *strikes an attitude.* GAIL. *pays not the least attention to them.*)

Gail. (frightened). It wasn't a joke. She was on the point of sending for the police. Ten thousand francs. There were ten thousand francs in the bouquet. Ten thousand francs sent by young — what's his name; and she accuses me of having stolen them. (*Notices* BIC.) Ah!

Jennie (to GAIL.). Allow me to introduce Monsieur Bicoquet.

Gail. Well, yes — by and by. But the bouquet first. What have you done with the bouquet that I just gave you?

Jennie. That bouquet! Do you dare to speak of it?

Gail. It is in your room, is it not?

Jennie. No, sir; it is not in my room. I threw it out of the window.

Gail. What? When?

Jennie. I threw it away, sir; because I knew where it came from. Do you understand, sir? I know all ——

Gail. You have thrown it away! (*Enters precipitately into* JENNIE'S *room,* R.)

Jennie (disappointed). Did you ever see anything like it?

Bic. (quickly). Did you notice, madame? It is impossible that you should not have noticed. He had a hat ——

Jennie. No; I was too much occupied.

Bic. But the hat was gray.

Enter GAILLARD, R.

Gail. (crosses to door, C., *and calls).* Pauline! — don't she hear? — Pauline!

Jennie (exasperated). O, what shall I do?

Enter PAULINE, *who keeps near door,* C.

Gail. Quick! Run down and ask the porter if he has picked up a bouquet which was thrown from the window.

Pauline. Yes, sir. (*Exit,* C. — GAIL *returns down,* C.)

Bic. I think I'd better go up again. (*Crosses towards* C.)

Gail. (stopping him). Remain, sir, I beg you.

Jennie (to GAIL, *who does not listen).* In a quarter of an hour; — pay attention to what I say, sir; — in a quarter of an hour I'm going to leave this house, to find a refuge with my aunt. You will never see me again. Don't try to defend yourself — it will be useless. Send Pauline to me when she returns. (*Bursts into tears, and exit door,* R.)

Bic. (to GAIL). Well, sir?

Gail. (to PAULINE, *who enters).* Well?

Pauline. The porter has not seen the bouquet, sir.

Gail. Very well. I will attend to the rest. Go to your mistress' room — she wants you. [*Exit* PAULINE, R.

Bic. (*heroically*). Yes, sir, I acknowledge it; it's all true. You have stolen my happiness along with the woman I love; and I, in return, have stolen ——

Gail. O, bother that at present. Bicoquet, I believe —

Bic. James Bicoquet.

Gail. (*crossing to secretary*, R.). Yes, yes, all the same to me. (*Aside.*) I must pay somehow. (*Taking money-drawer from the secretary, and putting it on table, pushes off hats with the drawer.*) In the drawer, 4950 francs. In my portemonnaie and in my pockets (*counting money*), 627. (*Feels in all his pockets.*) What is this? — some sous — 627 francs 30 sous. (*Figures in pocket-book.*) That makes 5577 francs 30 centimes. Not enough to pay ten thousand. (*Calculating.*) The remainder is — (*To* BIC.) Have you 4422 francs 70 centimes about you?

Bic. 4422 francs?

Gail. Yes, and 70 centimes. If you have it, lend it to me.

Bic. (*explosively*). Well, and I should like to know why?

Gail. Why?

Bic. Yes.

Gail. Because there are situations in which a man of pleasure always expects another man of pleasure to have 4000 francs about him. I am in one of these situations. There were 10,000 francs in the bouquet.

Bic. O!

Gail. Yes, and she demands them, and accuses me of stealing. You understand that I cannot go and tell her that my wife threw the bouquet out of the window. I must pay them — not to-morrow, nor in an hour, but immediately.

Bic. (*much interested*). Yes, I understand.

Gail. (*shaking his hand*). Then lend me the money.

Bic. How much did you say — 4000 francs?

Gail. 4422 francs 70 centimes.

Bic. (*slowly counting on his fingers*). 4422 francs 70 centimes. I haven't got it.

Gail. (*angrily*). Then why didn't you say so at once. How much have you got? Have you any money at all?

Bic. (*drawing money slowly from pocket*). I have. 43 francs 25 centimes.

Gail. Let's have them. (*Figures in book.*) That makes 5620 francs 11 sous. Haven't you any more? Look.

Bic. (*low, and trying to conceal some bills, which he shows to audience*). I have still a note for 1000 francs, and one of 500 — but ——

Gail. (*who has heard*). Give them to me. (*Snatching them.*) Are you afraid? I am known, sir! (*With pride.*) I have a name on change. I am one of those who pay, sir; who always pay — till just this moment.

Bic. Listen to me, sir. I hate you!

Gail. Well, sir; and I. Do you think that after having discovered you in a tête-a-tête with my wife at this hour, that I don't intend to ask an explanation? But not now, sir; not now. How did the figures stand?

Bic. (furious). I know nothing about it.

Gail. (equally furious). Well, sir, I'll tell you — 7120 francs 50 centimes. (*Calmer.*) Who shall I apply to next? My wife? She will profit by the occasion to inform me she has run into debt. Ah, the chambermaid! (*Rings.*) Pauline! Pauline! (*Enter* PAULINE, R.) Why don't you come sooner when I ring?

Pauline. But, sir, I was with madame. She doesn't know which dress to put on to seek a refuge with her aunt.

Gail. With her aunt?

Pauline. Yes, sir. Is it possible that you don't know?

Gail. Well, well, we'll see about all that immediately. Tell me, Pauline, have you saved any of your wages?

Pauline. I have 500 francs, sir.

Gail. Go get them for me. At the same time, step in and see the cook — she ought to have saved something also. Ask her for it on my account. At the same time get what there is left of the housekeeping money. Tell her to give you all the money she has — do you understand? — all she has.

Pauline. Certainly, sir. [*Exit*, C.

Gail. (*fumbling in his pockets*). You have nothing more left, have you, sir?

Bic. (*impatiently*). No, nothing, at all, sir.

Gail. And to think that all this has happened because there are some men in the world foolish enough to send 10,000 francs to a woman in that manner ——

Bic. Little what's-his-name ——

Gail. And he calls himself a gentleman. Instead of employing his fortune nobly — or rather — I mean instead of keeping his 10,000 francs — (*Fumbling in pockets.*) You are quite sure that you have nothing left, sir?

Bic. But I told you, sir ——

Enter PAULINE, C., *napkin in one hand, with her savings, and pitcher in the other, in which are in silver the savings of the cook.*

Pauline. Here are my 500 francs, sir. (*Gives napkin to* GAIL., *who passes it to* BIC. — GAIL. *figuring all the time.*) Here is the house money — 259 francs 90 centimes; and here are the cook's savings — 1950 francs.

Gail. (*book and pencil in hand*). 1950 francs saved, and she has been here four months; and when she came she hadn't a sou — twice her wages. Well, I'll reserve it. Pauline, put it all there. (*Points to table.*)

Pauline. The cents also, sir? (*Goes to table.*)

Gail. Everything — all. Put it all there.

Pauline. Here it is, sir. (*Spills money from pitcher into drawer, and exit.* BIC. *picks up what money has fallen on table and floor.* GAIL., *calculating, crosses,* R., *and they are on each side of table.*)

Gail. (*figuring*). How much does that make, in all — that makes 9823 francs 45 centimes. I must carry her that. Haven't you any more money about you?

Bic. (*sitting* R. *of table*). Listen to me. I hate you.

Gail. (*still figuring*). So you told me; but that is all reserved. I keep that back along with the cook's savings.

Bic. (*grandly*). I hate you. But I cannot see a gentleman in such perplexity without doing all I can to extricate him. (*Rises, and takes piece of money from the pocket of his waistcoat.*)

Gail. (*aside*). I knew he had something more.

Bic. (*passes piece*). There, take it.

Gail. I was sure of it. (*Examines piece.*) What is this — twenty sous?

Bic. (*nobly*). A piece with a hole in it — a keepsake — and I give it to you.

Gail. Well, that makes 9824 francs 45 centimes. (*Puts the sum into his handkerchief. — The money ought to be composed of the oddest kind of money.*) I will carry her this; and if she is not satisfied, I will offer her your watch. [*Exit,* C., *with money.*

Enter JENNIE, R., *dressed to go to her aunt.*

Jennie. Is he gone?

Bic. (*who has picked up hats, and replaced them on table*). Come in, madame, come in. Have no fear. We need trouble ourselves no longer. I have lent him money.

Jennie. Where is he now?

Bic. Need you ask?

Jennie. Again!!!

Bic. He took a large sum of money bank-notes, gold, silver, and my twenty sous piece — wrapped them all in a handkerchief, and carried them all to her.

Jennie. (*pulling on gloves furiously*). To my aunt's immediately. You will conduct me there, sir?

Bic. O, certainly; with pleasure. Where does she live, madame?

Jennie. At Rambouillet.

Bic. At Rambouillet? (*Suddenly recollects that he has no money.*) O, goodness!

Jennie. Well, what *is* the matter.

Bic. (*in despair*). Just my luck. For once in my life I have a chance to run away with a married woman, and — I've lent the husband all my money.

Jennie. What did you say, sir?

Bic. But that makes no difference. We will walk; and when we are tired we will take turns in carrying each other, so that one of us will be resting all the time.

Enter GAIL, *with a cap under his arm.*

Gail. (*to audience*). She refused the watch. She has some good traits left.

Bic. (*taking cap from him*). Allow me to relieve you, sir. I will put it with the others.

Gail. (*astonished*). What's that?

Bic. There must be a hat factory up stairs. (*Examines cap, and puts it with others.*)

Jennie. Another one!

Bic. Well, it's all the same to me. I've sworn never to love more.

Gail. (*to* JENNIE). And where are you going now, my dear?

Jennie (*dignified*). I am going to my aunt's. This gentleman will accompany me.

Gail. This gentleman?

Jennie. Yes, sir — the only protector I have left.

Gail. (*amiably*). But he cannot accompany you. since they are expecting him up stairs.

Bic. Expecting me?

Gail. (*low to* BIC.). And this time I swear I will not disturb you again.

Bic. Waiting for me? What strange people we men are. Now that she's waiting for me, I've no desire to go. (*Looks at watch.*) Twenty minutes after twelve. I think the best thing I can do now is to take a carriage and go home to bed. Yes — (*saluting with* GAIL.'s *hat, to* GAIL.) — I was going to take your hat again — the force of habit. (*Takes his own hat.*) Once more, adieu. Remember me — I'll remember you.

Gail. Good night, sir. (*Exit,* BIC., C. — GAIL. *passes him out.* — JENNIE *crosses,* L.)

Gail. (*near* JENNIE). Well, Jennie, dear.

Jennie. Well, what?

Gail. (*caressing*). You heard what the gentleman said. It's twenty minutes after twelve, and ——

Jennie. After what has passed, do you dare hope?

Gail. Do you really mean to leave me?

Jennie. I don't wish to make any scene, because it spoils my complexion to weep. But as for pardoning — never!

Gail. Never?

Jennie. Never! Never!! Never!!!

Gail. (*coaxing*). Never is a long time, and ——

Jennie. Well, there, I want to be good, and I will forgive you when ——

Gail. When what?

Jennie (*laughing*). When you bring me back this bouquet — this famous bouquet — which has cost you ——

Gail. (*bitterly*). 10,000 francs.

Jennie. 10,200 francs, my dear.

Gail. Yes — that's very true. I forgot the 200. (*Door bell rings violently.*)

Jennie. Who can that be now?

BIC. *appears at the door, the bouquet in his hand.*

Bic. Here's the bouquet! Here's the bouquet!

Gail. The bouquet? Yes. Come in, come in.

Bic. (*entering*). I declare, if this story should be related in any paper, nobody would believe it — and still it's the truth. A coachman was passing the door ——

Gail. (*looking at bouquet*). Just permit me to see the letter. It is there. You may go on now, sir.

Bic. A coachman was passing the door. I stopped him, and told him to take me home. "If it's all the same to you," said he, "would you like an adventure? Let us walk up and down before this house." His language made me suspicious — the more so that, while speaking, the coachman pressed to his heart, and covered with kisses, a bouquet that I seemed to remember. "Where did you get those flowers?" said I to him, in tones of authority. "Just now a lady threw them to me out of the window." He had scarcely finished, than I seized the bouquet, and rang at your door. Now, sir, take it.

Gail. (*takes bouquet*). The letter! Here it is — attached with a pin. Young what's-his-name gives a great deal of money to women — but he is orderly in his habits.

Jennie. Quick, my dear, quick!

Gail. (*taking letter, and giving bouquet to* BIC.). "Mademoisselle Antonia Brunet" — that s the one. (*Opens the letter.*) How's this? — no money. (*Reading.*) "My dear girl, I am glad that you applied to me for the 10,000 francs, but unfortunately I cannot send them at present. I regret — " (*Furious.*) And this man calls himself a gentleman. A lady applies to him for 10,000 francs, and he doesn't send them. (*Reading.*) "I regret it exceedingly — " (*Spoken.*) And I, too. (*Reading.*) "But to show you that I still think of you, I send —— "

Jennie. You see he sends something.

Gail. (*finishing the letter*). "I send you a front seat for the theatre."

Jennie. Just what I wanted this evening.

Gail. Yes; but where is this ticket?

Bic. (*taking ticket from bouquet*). Here — attached with a pin.

Gail. He don't send any money to women — but his habits are orderly.

Bic. (*examining ticket*). Unfortunately it's for this evening, and it's now a half hour after midnight.

Jennie. O, dear; how unfortunate!

Gail. (*takes ticket, and examines it at arm's length*). 10,000 francs.

Bic. (*to* GAIL, *and glancing at* JENNIE). I will not profit by your misfortune to disturb you, sir, but you owe me 1543 francs 25 centimes. Now, if you wish, you may pay me twenty sous a day. Every day, for 1543 days and a quarter, I will visit madame, and she shall give me a franc at each visit.

Gail. (*gayly*). You are pleased to be facetious, sir. You shall have your money to-morrow. (*To* JENNIE.) To-morrow evening, my love, we will go to the theatre.

Jennie. But you can't afford it after this expense.

Gail. Well, it's only 10,000 francs, after all. (*Enthusiastically.*) If the news continues to be bad for a week I can easily regain that.

Bic. Till to-morrow, my friend. [*False exit.*

Gail. Till to-morrow. But one thing, my friend, I hope you will promise me.

Bic. And what is that?

Gail. Promise me not to return again this evening.

Bic. I promise you. But there is still one thing more. There are two gentlemen waiting outside.

Gail. Two gentlemen?

Bic. Yes, two gentlemen — who have just left up stairs, and who cannot go away, because their hats are here. I entered alone, but, if you wish, I will call them in.

Gail. No, no.

JENNIE *takes gray hat and cap, and carries them to* BIC.

Bic. Thanks. And to repay you for the pleasure of the evening, I shall take the earliest opportunity of sending madame a "Bouquet."

GAILLARD. JENNIE. BICOQUET (*with hats in hand*).

SPENCER'S UNIVERSAL STAGE.

No. 32. **THE CHRISTENING.** A Farce in One Act. By J. B. Buckstone. 5 Male, 6 Female char.

" 33. **A RACE FOR A WIDOW.** A Farce in One Act. By Thos. J. Williams. 5 Male, 4 Female char.

" 34. **YOUR LIFE'S IN DANGER.** A Farce in One Act. By J. M. Morton. 3 Male, 3 Female char.

" 35. **TRUE UNTO DEATH.** A Drama in Two Acts. By J. Sheridan Knowles. 6 Male, 2 Female char.

" 36. **DIAMOND CUT DIAMOND.** An Interlude in One Act. By W. H. Murray. 10 Male, 1 Female char.

" 37. **LOOK AFTER BROWN.** A Farce in One Act. By Geo. A. Stuart, M.D. 6 Male, 1 Female ch.

" 38. **MONSEIGNEUR.** A Drama in Three Acts. By Thomas Archer. 15 Male, 3 Female char.

" 39. **A VERY PLEASANT EVENING.** A Farce in One Act. By W. E. Suter. 3 Male char.

" 40. **BROTHER BEN.** A Farce in One Act. By J. M. Morton. 3 Male, 3 Female char.

" 41. **ONLY A CLOD.** A Comic Drama in One Act. By J. P. Simpson. 4 Male, 1 Female ch.

" 42. **GASPARDO THE GONDOLIER.** A Drama in Three Acts. By Geo. Almar. 10 Male, 2 Female char.

" 43. **SUNSHINE THROUGH THE CLOUDS.** A Drama in One Act. By Slingsby Lawrence. 3 Male, 3 Female char.

" 44. **DON'T JUDGE BY APPEARANCES.** A Farce in One Act. By J. M. Morton. 3 Male, 2 Female char.

" 45. **NURSEY CHICKWEED.** A Farce in One Act. By T. J. Williams. 4 Male, 2 Female ch.

" 46. **MARY MOO; or, Which shall I Marry?** A Farce in One Act. By W. E. Suter. 2 Male, 1 Female char.

No. 47. **EAST LYNNE.** A Drama in Five Acts. 8 Male, 7 Female char.

" 48. **THE HIDDEN HAND.** A Drama in Five Acts. By Robert Jones. 16 Male, 7 Female char.

" 49. **SILVERSTONE'S WAGER** A Comedietta in One Act. By R. R. Andrews. 4 Male, 3 Female char.

" 50. **DORA.** A Pastoral Drama in Three Acts. By Chas. Reade. 5 Male, 2 Female char.

" 51. **BLANKS AND PRIZES.** A Farce in One Act. By Dexter Smith. 5 Male, 2 Female char.

" 52. **OLD GOOSEBERRY.** A Farce in One Act. By T. J. Williams. 4 Male, 2 Female ch.

" 53. **WHO'S WHO.** A Farce in One Act. By T. J. Williams. 3 Male, 2 Female char.

" 54. **BOUQUET.** A Farce in One Act. 2 Male, 2 Female char.

" 55. **THE WIFE'S SECRET.** A Play in Five Acts. By George W. Lovell. 10 Male, 2 Female char.

" 56. **THE BABES IN THE WOOD.** A Comedy in Three Acts. By Tom Taylor. 10 Male, 3 Female char.

" 57. **PUTKINS: Heir to Castles in the Air.** A Comic Drama in One Act. By W. R. Emerson. 2 Male, 2 Female char.

" 58. **AN UGLY CUSTOMER.** A Farce in One Act. By Thomas J. Williams. 3 Male, 2 Female char.

Catalogue of Plays for Amateur Theatricals.

BY GEORGE M. BAKER,

Author of "Amateur Dramas," "The Mimic Stage," "The Social Stage," &c.

DRAMAS IN TWO ACTS.

SYLVIA'S SOLDIER	3 Male,	2 Female Characters.	
ONCE ON A TIME	4 "	2 "	"
DOWN BY THE SEA	6 "	3 "	"
BREAD ON THE WATERS	5 "	3 "	"
THE LAST LOAF	5 "	3 "	"

DRAMAS IN ONE ACT.

STAND BY THE FLAG	5 Male Characters.	
THE TEMPTER	3 "	1 Female Character.

FARCES.—Male and Female Characters.

WE'RE ALL TEETOTALLERS	4 Male,	2 Female Characters.	
A DROP TOO MUCH	4 "	2 "	"
THIRTY MINUTES FOR REFRESHMENTS,	4 "	3 "	"
A LITTLE MORE CIDER	5 "	3 "	"

FARCES.—Male Characters only.

WANTED, A MALE COOK	4	Characters.
A SEA OF TROUBLES	8	"
FREEDOM OF THE PRESS	8	"
A CLOSE SHAVE	6	"
THE GREAT ELIXIR	9	"
THE MAN WITH THE DEMIJOHN	4	"
HUMORS OF THE STRIKE	8	"
NEW BROOMS SWEEP CLEAN	6	"
MY UNCLE THE CAPTAIN	6	"

FARCES.—Female Characters only.

THE GREATEST PLAGUE IN LIFE	8	Characters.
NO CURE NO PAY	7	"
THE GRECIAN BEND	7	"

ALLEGORIES.—Arranged for Music and Tableaux.

LIGHTHEART'S PILGRIMAGE	8 Female Characters.
THE WAR OF THE ROSES	8 " "
THE SCULPTOR'S TRIUMPH	1 Male, 4 Female Characters.

MUSICAL AND DRAMATIC ENTERTAINMENTS.

TOO LATE FOR THE TRAIN	2 Male Characters.		
SNOW-BOUND; OR, ALONZO THE BRAVE AND THE FAIR IMOGENE,	3 "	1 Female Character.	
BONBONS; OR, THE PAINT-KING	3 "	1 "	"
THE PEDDLER OF VERY NICE	7 "	Characters.	
AN ORIGINAL IDEA	1 "	1 Female Character.	
CAPULETTA; OR, ROMEO AND JULIET RESTORED	3 "	1 "	"

☞ Temperance Pieces.

THE LAST LOAF.
WE'RE ALL TEETOTALLERS.
A DROP TOO MUCH.
THE MAN WITH THE DEMIJOHN.
A LITTLE MORE CIDER.
THE TEMPTER.

Plays sent by Mail, postpaid, on receipt of 15 cents each, with the exception of "Snow-Bound" and "Bonbons," which are 25 cents each.

www.ingramcontent.com/pod-product-compliance
Lightning Source LLC
LaVergne TN
LVHW011138110826
845150LV00008B/2387

9781418193102